A Practical Guide To
SUCCESS
in the United States Air Force

Rodney "Q" Phillips
Chief Master Sergeant, USAF, Retired

ISBN: 147529509X
ISBN-13: 9781475295092

ACKNOWLEDGMENTS

I would like to extend a tremendous "thanks" to my colleagues, supervisors, peers, subordinates, and fellow members of the armed forces who inspired me to put pen to paper to produce this collection of experiences. I especially would like to thank my family (Ange, DaMani, Malique, and Aiyanna) for their patience and support while I spent countless hours writing and editing.

I dedicate this book to the men and women of the armed forces, of both the United States and our allies, for their commitment, dedication, selfless service, and sacrifice. I pray that God continues to bless you and watch over you and your families.

Phillips family photo: (left to right) DaMani, Rodney, Ange, and Malique. (center) Aiyanna.

TABLE OF CONTENTS

PREFACE

Without a doubt, each of us uniquely determines the level of success we achieve. This level of success directly reflects the amount of time and effort we exert toward our goals. However, a few common facets of our behavior and attitude help turn our goals and aspirations into reality. For instance, growing up in Calhoun, Georgia (a small town not particularly known for its contributions to the armed forces and lacking many of the opportunities my service afforded me), I knew I would not spend my adult life there. In fact, early in my middle school years, I made up my mind that I would leave as soon as I graduated from high school.

Although I had not worked out the specifics, I was content knowing I would go somewhere someday, even without knowing where "somewhere" would be. Then, during my sophomore year of high school, I decided the Air Force would be my way out. I remember mentioning to family and friends, on several occasions, that I would join the Air Force in a couple of years. Each time, the response was practically the same: "You're not going anywhere."

At times, I even had my future predicted for me: "You ought to get one of those good paying jobs at one of the local carpet mills. I hear they pay well and have good medical benefits." Besides, except for a few people, everyone I knew had chosen to stay in Calhoun. Some who had received scholarships to attend prominent colleges and universities to play sports had only left Calhoun for one or two semesters and had come right back.

On the surface, I may appear to disdain life in Calhoun. Absolutely not! I take pride in being from Calhoun. That's where my roots are. Indeed, the experiences I had there definitely helped mold me into the person I am today and fueled my motivation to be successful in the Air Force. At many points, especially early in my career, I spent a considerable amount of time hoping the actions I took and things I accomplished would shed a positive light on my hometown and make my fellow Yellow Jackets proud. It is my prayer that I did just that.

That said: surely, I'm not the only person who has ever been eager to leave home to explore the world and experience things outside the town where he or she grew up. I would venture to say many of us may not be able to define what we want to do, where we want to go, or what we want to become. But, one thing is certain: we want to succeed.

Because paths to success vary, I can neither promise you a magic formula to become a chief master sergeant (the top 1 percent of Air Force enlisted personnel) nor directly tell you how to catapult past any obstacles currently in your way. However, I'm confident this book will be a practical guide to your success, whether you aspire to reach the top 1 percent or elect to measure success in a different way (e.g., getting an associate's, bachelor's or master's degree, completing a Ph.D. program, obtaining a certification in your specialty, becoming a well-rounded officer, retiring or separating from the service at a certain grade).

To me, success in the Air Force meant knowing what I was capable of doing, setting realistic, achievable goals and not letting anything or anyone stand in the way of obtaining the very best outcomes. Learning to identify and fully exploit my talents, both inherent and acquired, allowed me to devote all of my time, energy, and effort toward whatever I did. As a direct result of my efforts (and the help of some great people) success became a common theme and contributed to the type of leader, mentor, supervisor, follower, dad, husband and overall person I am today. My successes didn't come without sacrifice and unimpeded determination. Several first-ever feats came as a result of my willingness to take risks others would not dare. Fortunately, my studied approach to addressing challenges not only proved successful but also provided the motivation my subordinates, peers and supervisors needed to offer their support and follow my lead.

I'd be remiss if I didn't mention my success with maintaining a close relationship with my family while fulfilling my duties and responsibilities as an Airman. Without a doubt, staying focused and motivated to achieve my goals and aspirations would not have been possible without their sacrifices, unwavering support, and continuous encouragement.

Using my more than 24-year Air Force career as the backdrop, I took a closer look at significant periods in my life and assessed how I was able to succeed during those periods.

In this book, I offer you the results of my reflection and a few tips on how you can also succeed in the Air Force. To that end, I have carefully assembled a few tried and true principles I'm convinced will help you in your journey. Each section is based on ideas and approaches, extracted from my experiences that are designed to shore up your motivation and serve as reference points to help you deal with many twists and turns you're sure to encounter throughout your Air Force career.

Through a collection of personal stories, I offer you a combination of related concepts and real-life anecdotes to help you easily remember the premise of each and help you explain what you have learned to others. Each account is my interpretation of the events that took place. I omitted names and locations, in some cases, and replaced them with generalities to extend the expressed points of view to the entire enlisted corps.

Although I had to vary each story's length to fit the context, the length does not indicate the story's importance or impact. I've also included the insight of some of the most intelligent, accomplished service members our armed forces have to offer. I appreciated working with them in both leader and follower roles.

I'm confident you will find the information useful no matter if you are just beginning your Air Force career, halfway through your enlistment or nearing separation or retirement. Trust me; the information and insight will be beneficial to you regardless of your status.

To increase your chances of success in the Air Force, you will need to use as many tools and resources as possible. One very important and often overlooked resource is the advice of those who have already succeeded. As you read through this book, I predict you will begin to replace some of my stories with your own.

I encourage you to share some of your own stories with others. You've probably already achieved many things that may help someone else get through something or provide a boost or the affirmation needed to complete a task. The key difference is whether or not you decide to do as I did and give back. You don't have to write a book. Instead, spend some time mentoring or speaking with others and showing them how things are done. Take a few minutes from your normal schedule to conduct a mentoring session at your workplace, visit a community center, a veterans' home or even participate in a panel discussion with Airmen who've just entered the Air Force. I'm certain you'll find them captivated by your inputs during their quest to gain insight into what they'll need to do to be successful. I'm sure your efforts will be appreciated.

Now is the time for you to raise your level of impact and influence. You have the potential to reach greater heights every time you encounter a challenge. Carefully study each challenge and assess what you need to do to increase your level of success. A key to increasing your level of success is following a practical guide to getting you there.

Enjoy!

KNOW THE BENEFITS

When deciding to join the Air Force, you most likely listened to a noncommissioned officer (NCO) at a recruiting station deliver his or her "pitch." Although you know you'll receive a decent salary, you should also know you will receive gradual pay increases upon promotion as well as annual cost-of-living adjustments and tax-free housing and food allowances. These benefits are just the beginning of the rewards the Air Force offers. As time goes by and you've demonstrated your commitment, you'll enjoy other great benefits, such as retirement pay, Thrift Savings Plan, and tuition assistance.

Successful service in the Air Force comes with benefits beyond those offered by many private sector employers. For example, according to the Air Force's official website, after 20 years of service, you'll be eligible for retirement pay. No payroll deduction is required. The amount you'll receive is based on your rank at the time of your retirement, number of years served, and applicable retirement plan.

If you'd like to save a little extra cash per month, you may participate in the Thrift Saving Plan which allows you to place a portion of your monthly pay into an account similar to a 401(k) investment plan. Considered pretax dollars,

Thrift Savings Plan contributions reduce the amount of your income subject to tax and grow tax-free.

Available in several forms, too many to mention here, the Air Force also provides tuition assistance to pay for education, training, and hands-on experience to help you succeed. More in-depth descriptions of these and other benefits are available at www.airforce.com.

More than likely, most people don't enter the Air Force just for these few benefits. Many of us decide to join to improve our condition in life, to travel, or to follow in the footsteps of countless relatives and siblings. Regardless of the initial motivation to join the Air Force, a major key to your success is to remember where you came from.

REMEMBER WHERE
YOU CAME FROM

Where we're from defines not only who we are but also sets a solid foundation for whom we'll become. The countless lessons we learn about life from our family and friends play a large role in the actions we take or don't take in the Air Force. When faced with enormous challenges, you may hear the voice of someone from your past telling you to go the extra mile; don't give up; hang in there; keep your head up; don't quit; stay focused; or be strong.

On the other hand, if you've had a void of positive influences in your life, you may have to encourage yourself. You may have thoughts like, I'll show him (or her) I can make a difference; I am more than just a failure; I can make her (or him) proud; or I WILL amount to something. Regardless of the scenario, our past helps determine the actions we decide to take. Don't fret about these thoughts; they're residual parts of where we came from.

While you were growing up, more than likely, your parents did not know you'd join the Air Force and gain responsibility to successfully accomplish your duties. Therefore, your parents probably didn't have the foresight to prepare you for the armed forces. Fortunately, your Air Force supervisors and peers will instruct, guide, lead, and mentor you through your journey. Through these experiences, you'll develop the knowledge, skills, and abilities you'll come to rely on to increase your capacity. Removed from the place you are from, you'll be free to determine your level of success. Then, your progress will depend heavily on how well you balance your freedom.

BALANCE YOUR FREEDOM

As we move through various career stages, the Air Force affords us certain freedoms in phases. For example, at first you'll be prohibited from doing various things (wearing civilian clothes, driving your car, staying out past a specified time, calling your family, etc.). As you regain the right to do these things, you will probably appreciate many things you once took for granted. Additionally, as you regain privileges, you'll need to make good decisions because authority figures from your past may not be there to ensure you make good choices.

For maybe the first time in your life, you'll be free to do (or not do) whatever you please. For most of us, this freedom is extremely liberating. I remember my first encounter with such freedom shortly after being assigned to my first duty station at Chanute Air Force Base in Rantoul, Illinois. When I arrived in 1987, it felt great to stay up into the wee hours of the night watching the first television I purchased with my own money, enjoying my décor (done according to my budding tastes), and determining which bank I'd use.

A few times, staying up into the wee hours of the night caused me to be late for work; required my coworkers to do their jobs and mine until my arrival; and earned me some unscheduled trips to see my supervisors. Fortunately, it didn't take long for me to realize the detrimental effects of my irresponsible actions and I made the necessary adjustments early in my career. In contrast, I witnessed many of my friends' inability to balance their freedom—driving under the influence of alcohol, failing to fulfill financial obligations, starting a brawl at a local bar and many other things contrary to good order and discipline.

In each instance, the ramifications of their actions resulted in blemishes on their records for failure to meet Air Force standards. Some even met an abrupt end to their career. Your success in the Air Force is contingent upon your ability to balance your freedom to do (or not do) whatever you please with the ease of making good choices. As time passes and your Air Force career matures, the harder choices will soon come, and you will need to exercise sound judgment.

EXERCISE SOUND JUDGMENT

Acquiring sound judgment takes time and experience. The Free Dictionary defines sound judgment as the capacity to assess situations or circumstances shrewdly and draw sound conclusions. As in balancing our freedom, when we find ourselves in situations requiring sound judgment, we typically resort to what we're most comfortable doing or not doing. For instance, we decide to do the "right" thing based on how we had right and wrong defined for us during our upbringing. Another name for this definition of right or wrong is our moral compass. Our moral compass—a relatively simple instrument—is centered on our own sense of ethics, and we rely heavily on it.

Your success in the Air Force will be influenced by your willingness to not only use your existing moral compass but also to embrace the Air Force's moral compass—known as the Air Force Core Values—of Integrity First, Service Before Self, and Excellence In All We Do. Rooted in countless years of tradition and lessons learned, the Air Force Core Values provide a solid ethical foundation for its members. Embracing these three concepts and applying them to your everyday life will ensure you are on course to make it through the rigors of initial training and beyond.

During the initial Air Force training period (typically eight weeks), you'll encounter hundreds of individuals and participate in countless events and Air Force ceremonies where Integrity First, Service Before Self and Excellence in All We Do will be repeated over and over again. Like most new habits you practice, the more you are exposed to these concepts the more likely you'll be to conduct yourself accordingly.

In addition to its core values, the Air Force has a set of guidelines you'll be able to embrace and use to make better decisions: the Airman's Creed.

INTERNALIZE
THE AIRMAN'S CREED

Introduced in 2007 by General T. Michael Mosley, then Chief of Staff of the United States Air Force and championed by Chief Master Sergeant Rodney J. McKinley, then Chief Master Sergeant of the Air Force, "The Airman's Creed"—aka "The Creed"—reflects an Airman's pride in the role of air, space, and cyberspace power and the Air Force's commitment to supporting and defending the nation. The Creed's principles are designed to ensure we maintain a common focus, character, mindset, and spirit. When fully internalized, The Creed will make you proud to be affiliated with the Air Force. See for yourself:

THE AIRMAN'S CREED

I am an American Airman.
I am a Warrior.
I have answered my Nation's call.

I am an American Airman.
My mission is to Fly, Fight, and Win.
I am faithful to a Proud Heritage,

A Tradition of Honor,
And a Legacy of Valor.

I am an American Airman.
Guardian of Freedom and Justice,
My Nation's Sword and Shield,
Its Sentry and Avenger.
I defend my Country with my Life.

I am an American Airman.
Wingman, Leader, Warrior.
I will never leave an Airman behind,
I will never falter,
And I will not fail.

Up to this point, you've learned how your background influences your thinking and what you must be willing to accept as part of your everyday Air Force life. Though simplistic, these ideas are the keys to your success no matter how long or short your time in the Air Force. Armed with your internal moral compass, the Air Force Core Values, and The Creed, you have what you need to face the challenges that lay ahead, beginning with preparing for promotion testing.

PREPARE FOR PROMOTION TESTING

A long and prosperous career in the Air Force requires you to be prepared to take promotion tests; score well; and get promoted. In fact, because the Air Force has an established timetable which specifies when you should reach a certain rank, your longevity will depend not only on whether or not you get promoted but also when. As a NCO, well aware of the ramifications of not being prepared and taking into account that everyone has a different learning style, I routinely stressed to my peers and subordinates the importance of dedicating time to prepare for the annual, high stakes exam.

Unfortunately, I still heard some people proclaim they hadn't put a whole lot of time into studying, saying things like "I really didn't study a lot." or "I didn't study at all." or "I took off work about a week to cram." When I heard statements like these, I typically told people matter-of-factly that it was a good thing they hadn't gotten promoted because if they had, they could have easily made things worse.

Having taken several promotion tests, I know the level of commitment it takes to study the material and be able to recall what you know while in the testing room. Although the approach I explain in this chapter may be a little unorthodox, I can tell you that after getting promoted each time and being able to better care for my family, it was well worth the sacrifice.

Without going into any particulars about the promotion test itself (doing so is against Air Force policy and considered test compromise), I offer the following tips on how to prepare for the examination.

Ensure you have the latest copy of Air Force Pamphlet 36-2241, *Professional Development Guide* (PDG). Your commander's support staff will usually provide you with a copy of the PDG. You can also retrieve an electronic copy by visiting the Air Force Publications website at www.e-publishing.af.mil. Inside the PDG, you'll find references for everything you'll be required to do and know as a member of the Air Force.

If you've previously tested for promotion, compare the current PDG to any previous versions you might have. This cross-reference ensures you are aware of information that has been added or changed. Dramatic changes are seldom made to the PDG, because most of the information is static. For example, the historical information remains relatively the same for each version of the PDG.

Set up a regimen that fits your and your family's routine. This consideration is important because you'll devote many hours to studying and may find you're missing some activities and events like enjoying precious moments with your kids, participating in cherished memories with extended family and friends, etc. I remember spending many days confined to my mother-in-law's living room while my family spent those days shopping and taking in the sun and sites of Fort Walton Beach, Florida.

Read the PDG at least five times. Rereading five times may seem extreme; but if you do it, you'll begin to notice themes in the information that will help you recall the material later. However, don't just sit down and start reading; instead, pre-plan your study sessions for greater success using the following steps:

1. Determine the date you'll start studying. From that date, determine the number of days between that start date and the date you plan to stop studying before you take the promotion examination. It's fine if you plan to study right up until the test date, as long as you count that date too.

2. If you don't plan to study on weekends or holidays, subtract those days and any other days you don't plan to study from the total you came up with in step 1.

3. Determine the number of pages in the current PDG; remember that changes to the PDG may increase or decrease the page count.

4. Divide the number of pages in the PDG by the number of days you came up with in step 2. This resulting total is the number of pages you need to read each day to reach your goal. For example:

428 pages/90 days = 4.8 pages. Round the 4.8 pages up to 5.

5. If you plan to read the PDG five times as I suggest, multiply the number of pages you came up with in step 4 by five. Using our example from step 4 then, you'd need to read 25 pages each day (5 pages x 5 = 25 pages).

If you're also required to take the Specialty Knowledge Test (SKT), which gages how well you understand your job, perform the steps above to determine the number of pages you'll need to study each day. Then, add that number to the number of PDG pages you must study each day.

Consider commercial test preparation tools. An additional tool I used while preparing for promotion was commercial PDG and SKT software. Although the commercial software cost me nearly $200 each time, I found the tools helped me meet my goals and tested my knowledge and understanding of the PDG and SKT material. The hardcopy books were great, but the CDs were most useful because they afforded me an opportunity to take advantage of the time I spent traveling, waiting in line at various places, and even while lying in bed each night.

With this information, you're now ready to begin studying. If things prevent you from reaching your targeted daily studying goal, just add the amount of pages you missed to your next study session to stay on track. In addition, if you have more time than you initially planned or if you reach a certain spot and can't seem to put the book down, you can read more. Reward yourself for studying any extra pages, but don't use any extra milestones reached to skip a few days, especially if you don't have a good reason to deviate from your schedule.

Don't make excuses. Not allowing yourself to make excuses is more important than you might realize. For instance, after you've established your regimen, all sorts of things will most likely come up that could easily be used to justify putting off studying. Once you allow yourself to make excuses for not studying, chances are, you'll find new excuses in the future to keep you from honoring your commitment.

Combat the anxiety and other distractions. Having only one shot each year for promotion puts increased pressure on you to do all you can before the test date to prepare. Knowing that, I encourage you to channel 100 percent of your energy into achieving your goal. Remove any negative thoughts you might have of not getting promoted, such as not scoring high enough on the examination (which you haven't taken yet), and don't be concerned about factors of the promotion calculation you can't control (e.g., points for a time in grade, time in service, and board score). Thinking about these factors will just worry you too much and will produce unnecessary anxiety.

Additionally, if you are contemplating retirement or separation from the Air Force while you are studying for promotion, predetermine the amount of time you'll spend on each. I say this because if you're spending most of your time thinking about life after the Air Force, you can't devote 100 percent of your focus to promotion testing. Giving anything less than your undivided attention will negatively impact your results.

Maintain the best mindset. With the right mindset and focus, you may even be able to convince yourself that you really aren't studying but rather are reviewing material you initially learned early in your Air Force training. For example, when you arrived at basic training, your exposure to how the Air Force operates began. The lesson material and demonstration performance tasks the MTIs guided you through are integral parts of the promotion examination. Subjects like military history, customs and courtesies, drill and ceremony, and profession of arms were introduced as items you must know.

Other items like supervision, mentorship, and the assignment process were among the topics explained during your newcomer's briefings, leadership experiences, and daily encounters with those you work for and with. So, in essence, by the time you're ready to test for promotion, you've already been exposed to the basic information you'll need to know when you enter the testing room. With this mindset, leading up to the actual test date, your preparation can then center on reviewing the material rather than on learning it from scratch.

Make it personal. Take time to contemplate the benefits you'll be able to enjoy if you're promoted. You'll be able to buy that new car; take your spouse on the honeymoon you couldn't afford before; take your family on vacation, etc. Thinking along these lines will help you stay motivated and will help you in those times when you want to excuse yourself from your study regimen.

Reward yourself for reaching each milestone. Spend some time considering how you'll reward yourself once you begin to reach your study milestones. These rewards don't have to be elaborate or expensive. My rewards varied. On one occasion, I recall treating myself to a large chocolate frosty after reaching my session goal. On another, I bought myself a nice silk tie. After a while, you'll look forward to treating yourself, making the study experience even more enjoyable.

Live with the consequences. As I've explained, you'll need to devote time and effort if you want to reach your goals. If you don't, be prepared to live with the consequences. When I was studying for promotion to staff sergeant, one of my coworkers was studying for the same promotion. Of course, we weren't studying together because that's against the law, but we'd ask one another how the preparation was coming along and encourage each other to continue studying the material.

On one occasion, I asked my coworker if she'd studied the night before, and she responded, "No. I had to work last night." Before replying, I considered that she was a single parent and may have needed the additional income. However, I still told her she needed to take time to study. I even asked her if she had breaks during her shift. When she said she did, I told her to take the book to work and read a page, a paragraph, a chapter, anything between those breaks. From that point and up to the day we each tested,

I felt we were pretty good friends. A few months later, when the promotion results were released, things changed. When she found out that I'd gotten promoted and she hadn't, she stopped speaking to me.

Now, not speaking to me would have been fine if we'd only had to see each other on occasion. But, we worked in the same office, so we definitely needed to communicate. Our job was to provide travel services to customers, which required us to collaborate to ensure they received uninterrupted service.

My coworker's silent treatment went on for several weeks until I finally requested that our supervisor speak with her to determine what her problem was and encourage her to at least recapture our professional relationship. After speaking with her, our boss told me that she was upset that she hadn't been promoted and was distraught because she'd been in the Air Force a few years longer than I had.

Heeding our supervisor's request to at least return to speaking terms with me, my co-worker soon realized that, for the good of the office, she needed to get beyond the setback. Not too long after the intervention, we were able to return to a somewhat normal working relationship, but I was careful not to express too much enthusiasm or excitement about my promotion. I didn't go out of my way to suppress my feelings, but I did try to understand her feelings even though I didn't completely understand them. After all, how could she be upset about not getting promoted if she hadn't honestly devoted the time and effort into preparing?

So, don't be surprised if your subordinates or peers say they didn't really study for a promotion examination. Be ready to discuss proper study habits with them and encourage them to fully participate in the process. The good news is, regardless of whether you get promoted or not, you'll gain some critical knowledge and skill during your preparation. Your vigorous regimen will also help make you a more effective leader, manager, supervisor and mentor. While you can do many things that will increase your chances of getting promoted, I also encourage you to get involved in things you like to do for reasons other than promotion.

DO WHAT YOU LIKE

To be successful, we should do what we like and not do things just to increase our chances of getting a promotion. Unfortunately, I've often consoled individuals who felt let down because they had only participated in things they thought (or had been led to believe) would help them get promoted. Some even took leave from work to deal with emotional swings ranging from severe anger at the system to complete withdrawal to mild depression.

Several factors impact the number of people promoted each year, such as projected end strength numbers, accessions, separations, retirements, and force-shaping initiatives. These factors alone discount any notion a magic formula exists for getting promoted. Regardless, some people still sacrifice family, friends, and countless other things to pack their resume full of activities they're certain will place them head and shoulders above the rest and increase their promotion chances.

Rather than do things just for promotion then, I encourage you to do what you enjoy simply because you like getting involved in those things. By doing what you like, you'll get self satisfaction from your actions while executing them. In other words, you won't need to accumulate things in order to receive a reward later.

When I was a technical sergeant, I developed a keen interest in teaching. I just hadn't quite made up my mind about the capacity in which I would teach. I didn't know whether I'd teach at a technical training school or in a professional military education setting or even at a public school, part time. All I knew is that I wanted to find a way to do what I do best: talk. So, a few years later when I was promoted to senior master sergeant, I decided to change my career path and fulfill my dream of teaching.

I was motivated to become an instructor as a senior master sergeant for several personal benefits that didn't include promotion possibility:

- I had recently attended the Air Force Senior NCO Academy (SNCOA) where my instructor daily displayed his excitement about teaching.

- I would have the opportunity to spend 4 years in an area of the country where my family and I were enjoying ourselves.

- I would have a reprieve from another remote assignment. (I had just returned from my second.)

- I would be removed from the deployment cycle. (I had been on several deployments and wanted a break.)

- I would be able to interact with my fellow senior NCOs from all career fields and career paths, something my present career field didn't afford.

- I would become certified as an Air Force instructor.

- I could earn another Community College of the Air Force Degree.

- I would improve my ability to speak and present information to any audience, regardless of size and amount of advance notice.

As you can see, I chose to teach because I'd receive some personal benefit, but not necessarily a promotion.

There is nothing totally wrong with doing things that offer some personal benefit. The challenge is to strike a healthy balance between your own aspirations and the needs of the Air Force. Fortunately for me, the SNCOA needed instructors as much as I needed to improve my personal situation, and the outcome turned out to be a win-win for both. Keep in mind, up until this point, I had completed my fair share of non-voluntary assignments, so I had sacrificed when called upon to do so.

I encourage you to do those things you like without being too concerned that people will say you're only thinking about yourself. Most people, no matter the position or rank, will do whatever it takes to achieve the greatest benefit for their particular personal and family situation.

Some people may even advise you to do things that ultimately will best benefit them. For example, the day after being notified that I'd been promoted to senior master sergeant, I received a call from a chief master sergeant offering his congratulations. At first, I didn't know what to say. I was honored that he had taken the time to congratulate me, but I had not heard from this person since I'd worked with him when he was a senior master sergeant years earlier. Shortly after his congratulatory remarks, he began to advise me on what I'd need to do to make chief master sergeant. Mind you, I hadn't even put on senior master sergeant yet.

After listing the things I needed to do, he then shifted the conversation to an upcoming remote assignment at a particular base. He pointed out the vacancy was actually for a chief master sergeant. However, he felt strongly that, if I played my cards right, I could move into the job as a senior master sergeant, putting myself ahead of my peers and lining myself up to make chief master sergeant. At that point, I realized he had not done his homework before calling me. If he had, he would have known that I had recently returned from my second remote assignment. His

apparent motive made me listen carefully as I waited patiently for an opportunity to tell him about my teaching aspirations.

While he was telling me how wonderful the remote base was and describing in detail the freedoms that came with being assigned to this particular location, I silently wondered why he (as a chief master sergeant)

had not volunteered for this dream job. I successfully suppressed the eagerness to ask him why and began to tell him what I planned to do. As soon as I mentioned that I wanted to leave my career field and complete a tour as an instructor, he immediately started to dissuade me. He told me such a move would absolutely ruin any possible chance of my making chief master sergeant. In fact, he said he knew many people who had chosen such a path, and each person had retired as a senior master sergeant. His exact words were: "You will kill your career."

Undeterred, I listed the reasons why I felt teaching was a good idea, even if the benefits did not include promotion. I told him that I hadn't been in the Air Force 16 years yet and was on track to put on senior master sergeant in a few months. I also mentioned that the average time in service for most individuals who made chief master sergeant was 20 years. This being the case, I told him I'd still be on track to make chief master sergeant in the average time, even if I decided to do a four year instructor tour. The chief master sergeant then told me that he couldn't guarantee I would receive a promotion to chief master sergeant even if I stayed in my career field; congratulated me, again, on my promotion to senior master sergeant; and wished me well on my journey to become an instructor. As I did, base your decision on what's best for you rather than the possibility of receiving a promotion.

Ultimately, I did become a SNCOA instructor, doing very well as a teacher. I was even selected as the 2006 Chief Master Sergeant Billy R. Hunter, Air Force Senior Noncommissioned Officer Academy Instructor of the Year.

With this honor, and the help of some great people, I was promoted to chief master sergeant in the instructor career field, even though that was not my primary reason for teaching. So, my overall message to you is to do what you like for your own reasons rather than for the sake of increasing your promotion chances.

If you do what you like and balance your aspirations, you'll reach your personal and professional goals while meeting the needs of the Air Force. Then, you can put the knowledge, skills, and abilities you gain into action.

PUT YOUR KNOWLEDGE, SKILLS, AND ABILITIES INTO ACTION

Our success in the Air Force hinges upon the ability to put our knowledge, skills, and abilities into action. To help exploit these talents, in-depth instruction and guidance are provided at every step of the way. Whether it's how to properly affix ribbons to your uniform or how to correctly cup your hands while standing at attention, you'll be shown how to achieve the desired outcome. I'm convinced that is why I was so successful. If I can't do anything else, I can follow instructions.

After repeatedly following the instruction and guidance provided by others, most of your actions will become automatic, but will require deliberate practice. Before long, you'll be able to use what you learn to execute your duties and responsibilities at your own pace.

I'm sure, at some point in your career, you'll be told the amount of time it should take you to grasp a task and you'll also be restricted from doing several things at once. This is because many Air Force leaders place artificial restrictions on the amount of tasks subordinates can learn within a certain timeframe and oftentimes advise against trying to do too many things at once. Take most of that advice with a grain of salt. Such sentiment is usually based on their own experiences or ability and not on your capacity.

I understand why restrictions might be placed on someone who's unable to strike the appropriate balance, but I don't agree with a blanket rule. For instance, while learning new duties and attending college, I recall being told more than a few times the amount of coursework I'd be able to handle, mostly prior to or without any preliminary skill assessment.

Fortunately, I was able to multitask, but not without a tremendous amount of sacrifice. Time and again, I replaced precious time with my family and friends with long nights, weekends, and holidays learning processes and procedures, studying for exams, preparing for quizzes, reading regulations, writing extensive papers, practicing for speeches, creating and reviewing curriculum and finishing a host of other supervisor and instructor driven requirements. On one occasion, I spent 16 hours on a Saturday writing 12, eight to nine page papers needed to earn my final semester hour credits for a master's degree. I'm not advocating that you do the same thing I did, but I do believe you have to be the judge of your abilities.

After you have the knowledge, skills, and abilities, you'll decide whether or not you follow the instructions provided, ask for assistance, or simply do something else in a situation. In each of these instances, making the choices that impact your success will depend on how well you use what you've learned to eagerly accept challenges.

EAGERLY ACCEPT CHALLENGES

An eagerness to accept challenges is essential to your success in the Air Force. Plenty of things need fixing, streamlining, revamping, modifying, etc. so typically, there're several challenging opportunities to improve something every day. I encourage you to seek such opportunities within and outside of your organization. As a bonus, I'm sure you'll find that you enjoy these challenges.

The most difficult challenges won't just come to you; you'll have to seek them out. The best place to look is in areas where most people don't feel too comfortable. For instance, highly visible and high-stakes challenges typically scare many people because they fear the potential for failure. When taking on a challenge, don't think about or fear failure. If you do, you automatically put yourself in a situation where you'll be exerting less than 100 percent of your effort. Instead, some portion of your energy will be distracted by worrying. To combat the fear of failure, you can take several actions.

Think of yourself as having successfully completed the challenge before you start. This concept is called prediction. I consider it a self-fulfilling prophecy. If you see yourself as having succeeded, you will.

Devise your plan. Take time to walk through every process, person, resource, and situation that will lead to your desired outcome. Use this information to create a solid plan of action. Include, in great detail, not only what you plan to do but also what you will do if your plan does not go according to plan.

Get buy in. Gain support for your ideas and aspirations by allowing others to carefully examine the plan and provide input. Doing so will make them feel part of the process and increase your ability to reach the desired outcome.

Identify any barriers standing in your way. Notice I said barriers not hurdles. I use this term purposely because you want to approach these things as obstacles that <u>must</u> be removed from your path and not simply crossed over.

Learn the roles others will play in meeting the challenge. If people in those roles are unwilling or unable to do their part, you must take action. Unfortunately, some people will fixate on things that keep a team from achieving its goal. These people usually tell you how difficult the challenge is and launch into a litany of reasons why something can't be done, even before you start. When I'm presented with this "naysaying," I thank the person because somewhere in the detailed reasons why we can't do something are the reasons why we can. In fact, I use the phrase: "knowing why you can't will tell you why you can" to help remove barriers.

Display a positive attitude and focus on the collective efforts of others needed to achieve the desired

outcome. When leading a group of people to complete a challenge, you must convince them a good plan is the key to success. Maintaining a positive attitude and a sharp focus on the goal will help convince people to work together.

Although you might think everything will progress smoothly if you follow my advice to accept challenges eagerly, it doesn't always work that way. Because Murphy's Law is ever present, anything is possible. According to Murphy, if anything can go wrong, it will. An example of Murphy's appearance happened on the first day of a rapid improvement event during my career.

After several months of preparation, my office was set to host twelve subject matter experts from twelve separate world-wide bases to standardize how we executed a Department of Defense personal property movement program. Leading up to the weeklong event, I'd been careful to ensure the first day—our only chance to make a great first impression—went according to plan.

To enhance my chances of succeeding, I placed the needed presentation material on the conference room computer under my log-in and asked several of my co-workers to do the same. This way, if something unexpected happened to me, I had plenty of back up. Good thing I took these extra measures.

The morning of the event, I arrived at the office two hours before anyone else and again started a dry run. Everything went as smoothly as it had gone during my earlier runs. But, after removing my common access card from the computer,

I noticed the brass strip was barely attached. Feeling fortunate that it hadn't come off inside the computer, I quickly secured the strip and headed to the Information Technology office to see if one of the technicians could somehow reattach it.

Fortunately, a technician was able to reattach the strip. However, knowing this was only a temporary fix, I chose not to risk my common access card getting stuck inside the computer. Remaining calm, I stopped by a co-worker's office an hour later and asked her to retrieve the presentation material using her log-in, so we could begin as planned.

It wasn't until after we had successfully completed the event that I told the team what had happened. They were surprised, to say the least. In mentoring moments, I still use that story as an example of how preparation is tied to success and how you can't let barriers keep you from accepting new challenges.

As with Murphy's Law, especially when people are involved, a strong possibility always exists that someone will make a mistake or two or three. When you make mistakes, don't panic; use them as opportunities to learn.

LEARN FROM YOUR MISTAKES

On our quest for success in the Air Force, we have numerous opportunities to do a lot of work. And, the more work we do, the more likely we are to make a few mistakes. Fortunately, you'll only need to be concerned if the number of mistakes you make begins to outnumber the instances when you don't make any.

You're more susceptible to making mistakes when you don't prepare well enough to achieve your desired outcome. For instance, in a hurry to introduce a new idea or concept, some Air Force members I've known made mistakes because they didn't dedicate time to adequately plan. Instead, they concentrated their efforts on getting the task done so they could take credit for the accomplishment in a performance report and/or award package.

When haste to finish supersedes preparation, we end up spending a lot of time fixing problems. Time we proclaim we didn't have, in the beginning, to properly plan. To characterize these instances when we chose to defy the odds against success without proper planning, I've adopted and used a saying over the years to exemplify this point: "We usually don't have time to plan to get it right the first time, but we always find time to do it over."

In instances where you simply make a mistake, don't spend a lot of time worrying about it, blaming someone else, or making excuses; just chalk it up as a learning experience, keep your head up, move on, and stay motivated.

STAY MOTIVATED

We must be highly motivated if we want to succeed in the Air Force and reach new heights. The Air Force provides your basic needs, such as food and shelter, as a condition of your employment; however, you'll have to work hard and be motivated to obtain greater rewards. You'll also need to stay off the sidelines and become actively involved in what's going on around you.

True motivation means different things to different people, so you'll first need to determine what motivates you. Distinct from emotion, motivation involves having an incentive to do something. Whether it's working at the neighborhood food bank, shelter, or another community-focused arena; devoting a few hours tutoring local school kids; meeting a fitness or weight-loss milestone; or expertly executing your duties and responsibilities, you can find activities that will encourage you to exploit your talents and skills. Daily, seek those opportunities that require your expertise and warrant your input. In addition, look for ways to move beyond doing things only when you're prompted and/or in the way they've always been done.

As you rise through the ranks, your supervisors will expect you to have the increased experience and knowledge to take on greater responsibilities. No longer will you always be told what to do; instead, you'll be expected to have the self-motivation to get things done. Depending on the type of person you are, you may find it difficult to identify what fuels your self-motivation. To help pinpoint this source, you can do several things.

Identify your own strengths and weaknesses. Understanding yourself is a key component to fully employing your talents and collaborating with others. All too often, especially when things don't go according to plan, we look outside ourselves for motivation. Knowing your strengths and weaknesses will help you become more well rounded, increase your confidence, and enhance your ability to succeed.

Perform self-examinations frequently. Looking closely at yourself and what motivates you, you might actually find you don't need much outside influence. Although it's normal to compare your success and progress to that of others, you're unique. So, don't use a co-worker's milestone achievements to gauge your progress. Instead, set your own milestones and figure out how to motivate yourself to achieve them.

Frequent self-examinations will also prevent you from blaming other people for your own shortcomings as some may even do to you. Too often, you'll run across individuals who have Heisman trophies in Monday morning quarterbacking. In other words, people who criticize or pass judgment with the benefit of hindsight. These individuals are usually among the first to tell you what you should have;

could have or what they would have done in a particular situation after the outcome is known.

A better approach is to evaluate your impact and use your talents and skills to affect the outcome. Start with your own self-assessment of what you could or should have done and move on from there. Using this approach, you may even see how you could have picked up on some warning signs and exerted your influence before an issue or problem became unmanageable.

Forgo the status quo. Most everyone you'll encounter in the Air Force is ready, willing, and eager to tell you how things have always been done. No matter how new the task, you'll be given an overabundance of justification for how things operate and why that way, without a shadow of a doubt, is the absolute best and only way to do it.

Much of this justification will likely come from one of two types of people: (1) the person who was there when the decision was made to do things that way and helped create the process or procedure or (2) the person who accepted, without question, the rationale for the way things are operating and is fine with keeping things that way. The problem is, both types of people are "typically" not willing to change or give any credence to someone else's new ideas.

I'll be the first to say that changing for the sake of change tends to do more harm than good. However, if you aren't careful, you'll find yourself accepting the status quo for the sake of expediency, especially in areas where the margin of error is relatively small. To ensure you don't make changes simply for the sake of change, you need to keep several things in mind.

Ensure you clearly understand the current process before you change it. This is important because if you don't understand what needs to be done, you could easily make the situation worse. Take copious notes to capture the good and bad elements of the existing process. Using this information, carefully study the processes in place. Armed with this information, make adjustments and set things in motion that allow the new approach to produce the desired results.

Choose the right time to make positive change. On several occasions, especially during turnover sessions, I've heard many times, "We've tried everything, and this is the way it needs to be done" although I wasn't given an opportunity to inject my experience performing the tasks. Because I knew I'd soon be responsible for the tasks, I chose not to try and convince the person from whom I accepted responsibility to do anything different. Instead, I waited until the individual left for his or her new assignment to make positive change. Surely, we cannot always afford to wait till someone leaves to institute change. Instead, we must conduct a thorough review of each situation and base our approach on its results.

Do things that are indisputably excellent. When you have an opportunity to complete a task or exercise your judgment, do it so well that no one can dispute the excellence of the result. I encourage you to grasp this concept because, unfortunately, you'll more than likely encounter some people who don't have your best interest in mind. These people seem to only look for ways to point out what you're not doing or how your best efforts aren't quite good enough.

Additionally, they may find it impossible to consider, evaluate or support your idea or approach, no matter how well thought out and even refuse to cooperate when asked for their input to make the idea better. Instead, they say "No," regardless of how well you've presented your proposal. This problem happened to me when I was assigned to an organization that made transportation arrangements for thousands of armed forces personnel returning from their deployments at various overseas locations.

When I arrived, the team of professionals who'd been performing the function was in its last few weeks before returning to their home stations. As the new flight chief, I was on a crash course to learn how things operated, so I could assume responsibility. For two consecutive weeks, I spent nearly every waking hour making sure I understood the source of the reservation requests, the measures taken to screen and arrange transportation and the process to provide confirmation to the travelers before they started their journey.

Early on, everything seemed to be going according to what I'd been briefed—no major issues. But before long, it happened. One night, I received a call from my commander who said he'd been told by his boss that 34 personnel had come through the base; had flown to the states; and were now stranded with no follow-on transportation arrangements.

At first, I thought this situation could not be possible because aircraft were charted specifically to take returning personnel to their destinations. As it turned out, these people had indeed transited our base and so had many others prior to my being assigned to the location. Instead of receiving prearranged transportation, they'd been allowed to board a flight that happened to be headed to the states.

As the person in charge, on a mission to ensure something like this never happened again, I committed myself to finding out what happened so I could prevent recurrence. After critically reviewing the entire process, to include consulting with incumbents remaining from the previous team and reaching out to those stranded passengers to get their account of what happened, I determined several disconnects in the process were potential causes.

During these conversations, I discovered the initial reservation requests had never been sent to our office for booking. Instead, according to the leader, the traveling team had been instructed to board an aircraft destined for our base and once there, someone would assist them with getting to the states.

Armed with this information, I explained the situation to my leaders and offered what I thought to be the cause of the problem, only to have my findings disputed by the individual who was responsible for obtaining travel for the team before its members began their journey. The person declared, "We sent the reservation requests to your office but didn't get anything back." Upon hearing this, it struck me as odd that no one followed-up to see why the reservation requests sent had not been confirmed and returned.

Unfortunately, because the Travel Reservation Request process was somewhat unmanageable due to the absence of a standard process, I had no concrete way to combat the person's assertion so I began to focus my effort on preventing it from happening in the future. To begin, my team and I collected data on the various ways reservation requests were sent to our office from each location. We then created a standard reservation request form and sent a draft copy to each location we serviced for review and input. The process took about five weeks, during which time naysayers and others who didn't want to cooperate tried to stifle our efforts to standardize the process. Despite the difficulty, we were undeterred.

In the end, we developed a new process that immediately rendered indisputably excellent results. No more travelers made it through our base without their proper transportation arrangements. Soon, word began to spread throughout the theater and up to the headquarters that transiting our location was no longer a bad experience.

Travel Reservation Request process prior to comprehensive examination by Senior Master Sergeant Phillips and his team of professionals. As indicated by the stacks of paperwork, the process is somewhat unmanageable due to the receipt of numerous requests in many different formats and on varying timetables.

One vice wing commander put it this way during his visit to our office after we had successfully arranged travel for thousands of personnel without incident: "I remember being told at my orientation before coming here that leaving the theater through this location was an absolute nightmare." He also felt it necessary to thank us for ensuring he hadn't had to endure the chaos his predecessors encountered. This visit was a true testament of our unwillingness to accept the status quo and forge ahead with new ideas despite the people who resisted our changes.

We were successful in our commitment to make things better. I encourage you to do the same and to not settle for the current state of affairs if you're unhappy with it. Additionally, don't allow your dedication and determination to affect positive change to go unrewarded, especially when many people, including some of your superiors, don't fully support what you did. To ensure you enjoy the fruits of your labor, I encourage you capture your ideas and efforts by writing your own performance reports and award packages.

WRITE YOUR OWN PERFORMANCE REPORTS AND AWARD PACKAGES

Our ability to communicate well, especially in writing, is important to our career development. In fact, your writing ability influences your success in the Air Force. All too often, I've encountered individuals who hadn't dedicated the necessary time and effort to developing the writing skills needed to complete Air Force correspondence. Most evident was their inexperience with producing solid bullet statements for performance reports (AF Form 910, Enlisted Performance Report [AB-TSgt] or AF Form 911, Enlisted Performance Report [MSgt-CMSgt]) and award packages (AF IMT 1206, Nomination for Award). Knowing how to write effective bullet statements is vital to taking care of your subordinates and is essential to ensuring your own evaluations and awards best highlight your achievements. Although no magic formula exists for creating bullet statements, I offer my tried and true method that will help you catalogue your accomplishments as well as those of others.

An effective bullet statement must include the action, the result, and the impact of the action. Combined, these three ingredients paint a clear picture of the importance of your actions to the overall outcome. Your highlighted action doesn't have to be something you did all by yourself, but you should communicate that the action's overall impact would not have been achieved had you not done what you did.

If you've written essays in high school or college, you can start with the same concepts you used for those essays. Begin constructing the bullet statement by drafting a complete story of what happened. Don't attempt to edit while writing this draft because you will waste time and block your creativity. In fact, I've seen many people sit for hours on end either staring at a blank sheet of paper or starting and stopping several times in an attempt to create the perfect bullet statement on the first try.

Instead, follow these five steps and the examples provided:

1. Write down the action.

Example: SSgt Jacobs created a weapon of mass destruction (WMD) training program.

2. Describe the action in specific terms.

Example: SSgt Jacobs created <u>an outstanding three-phase WMD training program on unauthorized ordnance detection techniques in the deployed area.</u>

3. Add the result of the action.

Example: SSgt Jacobs established an outstanding three-phase MWD training program, <u>eradicated 300 military working dog obedience problem areas and trained 20 teams</u> on the technique of unauthorized explosive ordnance detection in the deployed area.

4. Identify the overall impact of the action.

Example: SSgt Jacobs established an outstanding three-phase MWD training program on unauthorized explosive ordnance detection in the deployed area. The program eradicated 300 military working dog obedience problem areas. Twenty MWD teams were trained and informed on the importance of detecting unauthorized explosive ordnance. <u>Over 8,000 personnel are now better protected from force protection threats.</u>

5. Pick out the key elements (action, result, and impact) and write them in bullet form.

Example: Created three-phase WMD training program; eradicated 300 problem areas/trained 20--protected 8K+ from FP threats

If you've effectively included the three elements in the bullet statement, it will be evident that without your actions, the mission would have been severely impaired or possibly would have failed.

The dictionary and thesaurus can help you creatively describe your actions. Be careful though. You may be tempted to use words that are not so common and find it difficult to gain support for what you've written. Instead, your leadership may scrutinize and ultimately reject the bullets you write. The good news, however, is that your leadership's feedback on the bullets you write will make you a better writer and improve your ability to write your own performance reports and award packages.

Although some supervisors may find it odd that you'd write bullets for yourself, don't be discouraged from doing so. Consider what the alternative might be if you didn't write your own bullets. Let's say you did a great job completing tasks and the outcomes are indisputably excellent. However, when you should receive proper recognition for your accomplishments, you receive nothing—no achievement medal, no commendation medal, no meritorious service medal.

When this happens, you may think your boss either didn't think you deserved to be recognized and rewarded for what you did or chose not to take care of you. But, the problem really may be that he or she just didn't have the writing skills needed to effectively put the action, the result, and the impact of your efforts on paper. So, you will miss out on an opportunity for recognition unless you have the writing skills and initiative to take care of yourself.

I actually saw this situation happen during my four month tour at an overseas location. I was assigned with 23 other members to a theater headquarters staff performing logistics functions. Near the end of our tour, after we'd accomplished a host of important tasks, our boss told us that, if we wanted to receive an award for our performance, we'd need to complete a draft and submit it to her for review, necessary modification, and submission to the command staff for final approval. She even gave us plenty of time to complete the required 22 lines.

Used to the concept of writing my own bullets, I was the first to capture my accomplishments and turn in the draft, well ahead of the suspense. A few more people took our boss up on the offer, but one technical sergeant didn't. When I asked him why he wasn't going to submit his draft, he exclaimed in a rather aggressive tone, "It's not my job to write the draft; it's hers. If she wants me to receive an award, she'll write it herself!"

At that time and even now as I describe the series of events to you, it didn't make sense that he'd reject her offer under this premise. Besides, there were 24 of us and only one of her. If she took time out of her already busy schedule to write everyone's award, she wouldn't have time to get her own work done. I attempted to get him to look at the situation a different way by stressing the fact that he was the one who stood to lose, but he rejected my rationale and refused to write the draft.

Now, I had no reason not to believe what he said. However, I do believe his inexperience with writing could have played a part in his decision to pass up the chance to receive an award for his performance. He'd been in the Air Force a few years longer than me and, in my opinion, should have known how to write. But, because he may not have been given the training or ever took the time to grasp the concept, he chose not to subject himself to potential failure or listen to anyone tell him that, as a technical sergeant, he should be able to effectively write bullets.

From this experience, I actually learned a valuable lesson myself: no one is going to take better care of you than you are. Your boss may not fully understand what you do each day or how well you do it. That's why the common Air Force practice is for you to provide inputs for your performance reports and awards to your supervisor. I'm simply encouraging you to go one step farther and write your own bullets. In fact, you can download the applicable forms from the e-publications website or use the template provided by your administrative staff. Fill out the form completely and give it to your supervisor. Your supervisor may look at you strangely when you write and turn in your own bullets the first time, but will soon come to expect it. At some point, your supervisor may even expect others to do the same thing.

If that happens, I encourage you to look out for others as well. Always be ready and willing to help other people write their performance reports and award packages. The better everyone can capture their accomplishments in writing the better off the organization will be. Doing so will definitely increase your ability to help others succeed.

HELP OTHERS SUCCEED

We all meet many people in our careers that have varying levels of skills and expertise. No matter whom you meet in the Air Force, chances are great that some will come to you for help in certain areas where your skills exceed theirs. Whether it's for assistance with writing or working their way through a difficult task or assignment, they'll more than likely need something from you. The better able you are to honor their requests, the more apt they are to tell someone else how you helped them. As you help more people, you will expand your knowledge, skills, and abilities.

Depending on the level you reach in the Air Force, you may find that you spend the vast majority of your time providing assistance with a wide range of issues. For instance, on one of my overseas assignments, I had the privilege of working with other organizations predominately consisting of United States Army personnel who were operating on an Air Force installation.

This situation presented many challenges because the culture of the Air Force and the Army are so distinctly dissimilar. For example, the Army gives its enlisted personnel a great deal of responsibility for accomplishing their mission. Soldiers determine what operations are required to complete a mission and search for areas in need of improvement regarding their organization's capacity to carry out future missions. This typically allows soldiers to take on challenges without waiting for approval or following a strict process.

On the other hand, the Air Force tends to set up processes and procedures for obtaining predetermined outcomes and repeatedly meeting expectations, resulting in a slower process with several approval levels. Not meant to imply either is better, there were several instances when the Army personnel needed to get things done quickly but oftentimes found themselves "trapped" (as they put it) in the Air Force's bureaucratic web.

Fortunately, I effectively used my interpersonal skills to help the Army personnel navigate through those difficult times and resolve any problems they encountered when trying to complete their mission on an Air Force base. In effect, I became their liaison. In doing so, I gained their trust and support. Our relationship grew even more when the Army personnel sought my assistance in gathering information, connecting their members with Air Force personnel, and translating the wide range of Air Force requirements into instructions they understood and became accustomed to following.

As your reputation for being able to help others grows, you'll soon be deemed by your subordinates, peers and supervisors as the "go to person." When this happens, you will be expected to help others at any time. This may take some getting used to but I'm sure you'll adjust to the humbling opportunity. My motto was and still is: "My job is to make the people around me better." With this idea as your motivation, I encourage you to always look for ways to help other people succeed.

As you rise through the ranks, especially up to chief master sergeant, you need to know not only where you can find the keys to your own success but also how to share those keys with others. So, while you still have time, put yourself in a better position to carry out this responsibility by developing strong leadership and management skills.

DEVELOP STRONG
LEADERSHIP
AND MANAGEMENT SKILLS

Our success as leaders, guides, and mentors is contingent upon how soon we develop strong leadership and management skills. Everywhere you look, plenty of opportunities to apply these skills will appear. Although proficiency in leading and managing usually comes from experience, you can do several things now to improve your ability to set proper examples for others and lead people in the right direction.

Seek and attend professional military education (PME) courses. When the time comes, be ready to spend between four and eight weeks in one of the Air Force's fine PME institutions. Having spent four years as an instructor, I can tell you that many students don't come to PME determined to improve their leadership and management ability. Instead, some students focus only on receiving an award, hoping it will increase their promotion chances. I encourage you instead to attend PME with the goal of being a more effective leader when you finish the course than you were when you began.

Attend a college or university. Officers must have a college degree to enter the military, but enlisted members don't. As an enlisted member, however, you should still pursue higher education while you're in the Air Force. The concepts you'll be introduced to while completing your degree will help you devise more effective solutions to problems; improve your ability to articulate your message (both orally and in writing); enhance your credibility among your peers, subordinates, and supervisors; and benefit you in other tangible and intangible ways.

I understand if you're not convinced that as an enlisted person you need to go to college. In fact, I used to think the same way. I recall one point in my career when I routinely debated with my supervisor the reasons why I didn't need to go to college. At the time I could pretty much find or quote every regulation reference needed to do my job. As far as I was concerned, I knew everything I needed to know. Boy was I in for a rude awakening.

After spending time at a few other bases and gaining more experience, I arrived at a point in my career where my long-standing assertion about not needing a college education met reality. One afternoon, shortly after finding out that I'd missed being promoted to technical sergeant by only a few points, a civilian coworker approached me. She didn't offer the usual condolences and encouragement to study harder next time, but rather asked me why I wasn't channeling my talent into a college degree.

Gleaning from my reaction to her question that I really didn't have a logical answer, she then told me she'd watched me work and wondered how much more effective I'd be if I funneled some of my energy toward investing in my future after the Air Force. For a moment, I didn't quite know what to say, so I didn't say anything. She continued by giving me a few examples of things that I'd done that had made her take note of my abilities—my confidence to take on any challenge, my writing skills, my ability to handle high-visibility situations, and a host of other things I hadn't considered. She summed up by telling me that I should take advantage of the time while stationed there to do something to improve myself.

In her words, it was evident that I took my responsibilities to the Air Force seriously, but I needed to focus some energy into my own self-improvement. From that conversation, I decided to attend college, a decision that resulted in three associate's degrees, a bachelor's degree, and a master's degree. Unfortunately, my decision to heed her advice didn't come until I'd been in the Air Force for 12 years.

Malique, son (front left), DaMani, son (front right), Helen, mother (back left), and Rodney (back right), after receipt of his Bachelor of Science degree from Troy University in Montgomery, Alabama on 15 December 2005.

If you also haven't convinced yourself that a college education is important, take my advice now and enroll. You'll definitely be glad you did. When you decide to pursue higher education, encourage everyone who'll listen to do the same thing. On several occasions, moving up through the ranks and after becoming a chief master sergeant, I took the time to encourage others to continue their education.

I once had the opportunity to participate in a panel discussion with a fellow chief master sergeant at a NCO Enhancement Seminar. While there, we fielded questions from and talked to the attendees about a variety of topics ranging from how to improve their leadership skills to how to write effective bullet statements. A major portion of the discussion was also about higher education.

Because the other chief master sergeant on the panel was senior to me, I yielded to his remarks first. Interestingly, his story began by taking us through his journey and valiant pursuit of acceptance into the Officer Training School located at Maxwell Air Force Base in Montgomery, Alabama. I remember he stressed the fact that after receiving his bachelor's degree, he really wanted to become an officer. For one reason or another, he kept getting turned down. Fortunately, he was able to pick up the pieces and rise to the top of the enlisted ranks. Evidenced by his promotion to chief master sergeant, he did some great things in his career as an enlisted person.

My story, on the other hand, was strikingly different. I prefaced my remarks by saying I'd never had the ambition to be an officer, which led to an awkward applause. Definitely, there is nothing wrong with becoming a well-rounded officer. I know several people who, after spending time as enlisted members, chose to attend or complete their college degree; obtained a commission and did very well. When asked, many of them said that their experiences as enlisted members helped them fulfill their duties and responsibilities as officers and provided a much broader perspective of the Air Force.

From that point, I expressed to them the importance of being good, solid role models for the enlisted corps and emphasized the importance of continuously focusing on personal and professional growth.

Then, I began to talk to them about the importance of getting a college degree. After hearing about my debates earlier in my career when I thought getting a college education was not such a good idea, they were visibly surprised. I took the opportunity to point out that it's never too late to equip yourself with the tools needed to improve yourself and to set a proper example for others.

Although the amount of time and effort it takes to set a proper example and serve as a guide to so many enlisted personnel is not fully compensated financially (in comparison to the pay officers receive), the satisfaction of knowing you've made a positive impact on their lives and careers is priceless! Even if you don't receive the privilege of serving as a chief master sergeant, seize every opportunity to broaden your abilities. Doing so will certainly help you put your life in the proper perspective—a perspective you'll need in order to deal with the challenges ahead, including one challenge that is present whenever human beings interact: conflict.

RESOLVE CONFLICT EARLY

We must develop an understanding of conflict and equip ourselves with the skills to deal with it. Merriam-Webster's dictionary defines conflict as "a mental struggle resulting from incompatible or opposing needs, drives, wishes or external or internal demands." Because we all have our own needs, wants, aspirations and desires, conflict is a natural result of human interaction. Disagreement on issues is inevitable; no matter if the conflict stems from determining whose idea best defines how to complete assigned tasks or when to begin a work shift. It's how you manage conflict that will ultimately determine your success in the Air Force.

Many theories for managing conflict exist and teach various leadership concepts. Regardless of which management theory you follow, I think it's important to fully understand the ramifications of your actions and the reaction of others involved before you act. If you don't, the conflict could escalate and warrant someone else's intervention.

For example, when I was an airman, my boss had to intervene in a conflict that involved a co-worker and me. While stationed at one particular base, I had the misfortune of working with an individual with whom I just couldn't get along. For about a month, we seemed to have at least two or three conflicts every day. Some of these incidents stemmed from our desire to display to those around us the superiority of our job knowledge.

Routinely, we'd race to work in order to get the best duty in the entire office: manning the customer service counter. This, in our minds, was the ideal place to work because it afforded the opportunity, each day, to learn more and more. I remember reading entire chapters of regulations so I could be prepared, just in case someone came into the office seeking assistance in any facet of my specialty.

Without advance notice of who'd come into to the office for help, we had to listen carefully to many types of scenarios, field a variety of questions, and provide the right answers the first time, every time. Because, if we didn't, the inevitable would happen: we'd interrupt one another's conversation with the customer to correct the mistake. Sometimes, we even went to the extent of calling one another's customers back to correct something we'd overheard that wasn't quite right (according to how we'd put it) or to clarify something we thought we'd heard.

Fortunately, the majority or our spats took place outside the presence of our customers. One particular day we were really at each other's throats. Our exchange on this day became so heated that our boss summoned us both into his office. When we were inside, he calmly directed me to close the door. After letting us stand there quietly for a few minutes, our boss said, "I don't know what's going on between the two of you, but I do know one thing. You will stay in this office until you've worked out your differences. I don't care how long it takes, but when you come out that door, I don't want to see or hear any more of this. If you don't resolve your differences, then we'll settle it my way!"

Fearing that we'd receive disciplinary action for disobeying an order or something, and after several minutes enduring each other's stalling tactics, we spent the next few minutes pointing out what we believed was fueling our inability to work together. As it turned out, we both were Type-A personalities and wanted to be in charge. As a long-term fix and to keep our records clean, we agreed to plan how we could share responsibilities and follow each other's lead in situations. From that experience, I also learned that resolving conflict and collaborating with others can only happen when those involved are willing to do a few things to lessen the negative impact.

Treat others with dignity and respect. Learning how and treating others with dignity and respect is very important to your success in the Air Force. Terms like fairness, teamwork and respect come to mind when I think about how my actions will ensure there is a harmonious relationship between me and those I come in contact with, no matter the setting or purpose. If you encounter someone who loves to sow discord, don't allow your instinct to react to the unacceptable behavior to overshadow your need to maintain dignity and respect for yourself and for others.

Display the level of courage needed to seek help with bringing the conflict to the attention of those who can help you resolve it. Sometimes, your attempts to resolve conflict at the lowest level will fail or make the situation worse. In those instances, don't hesitate to get someone else involved before things escalate to a level that will negatively impact your career or worse, result in someone getting physically hurt. Once the issues have been addressed, though, I encourage you to move on.

Address the source of your issue or frustration directly. After resolving several conflicts, I've found that the problem actually started somewhere else, mainly outside of the organization, and manifest itself in the workplace. This happened because one of the people involved didn't confront the person causing the issue but chose to come to work and flex.

On one occasion, I was confronted by my supervisor's boss in my boss' absence. He was seeking information from me on whether my boss had completed a key task needed to meet a critical suspense. Anticipating my boss hadn't, the supervisor asked me in a rather aggressive tone if I knew if the task was complete. Not knowing about the task prior to his mention, I told him I didn't know and continued to execute my assigned duties.

Displeased with my answer, he launched into somewhat of a rage expressing how he wished "people" would just do their jobs. At that point, I decided to let things cool down a bit before making my way to his office. After a review of what happened and a less than sincere apology, he revealed that he'd had a bad encounter at home before coming to work. Upon hearing his revelation, I politely asked him to keep his issues from home at home.

I encourage you to deal with the source of your frustration and don't deflect your issues to other people. Remember, if I didn't cause your issue and you're not asking me to help you solve it, don't bring it to me!

For these and many other reasons, it's important that you view conflict as an inevitable reality and develop the skills needed to work your way through it. Doing so will help you establish and maintain healthy personal and professional relationships, increasing your ability to embrace diversity.

EMBRACE DIVERSITY

The Air Force is a diverse organization filled with people from all walks of life. We must work with people every day who look and think differently than we do. Your willingness to embrace this diversity will be key to your success. For this reason, you'll be required to attend numerous orientation and refresher training sessions designed to help you look beyond inherent biases, so you can accomplish individual and collective goals.

Familiarize yourself with the dimensions of diversity that you'll encounter in the people you meet, including age, gender, physical ability, sexual orientation, experience, marital and/or parental status, religion, and race. I stress this point because you'll likely encounter people from places you've never heard of, like Calhoun, Georgia. I challenge you to spend time with other people, so you can learn more about them and they can learn more about you. During these exchanges, you'll both find out some good and not-so-good things about each other, both personally and professionally.

Although most relationships among Air Force personnel tend to be professional, I encourage you to develop personal relationships as well. These relationships can be developed during unit functions, sporting events, and other activities.

Provided these personal relationships adhere to Air Force standards, they will help foster the teamwork and camaraderie needed to enhance your organization's ability to accomplish its mission. Cultivating personal relationships will also help you understand other people's strengths, rationale for decisions, and even differences in appearance.

During a lesson I taught on diversity, one of my female, African-American students shared an odd encounter she'd had with a lady who had grown up in a rural town consisting of only Caucasian people. The lady told my student that she'd heard stories about African-Americans, but had never personally seen any during her school years. It wasn't until the lady had arrived at basic training that she actually saw an African-American. The lady revealed that the texture of an African-American's hair was the most puzzling thing she'd heard about and wanted to confirm. Not knowing how her proposal would be received, the lady told my student she'd understand if she rejected the request but asked, "May I touch your hair?"

Taken aback at first by the request, my student carefully took us through her thoughts when the lady made her request. First was disbelief. She couldn't believe this was a genuine request and not some plot against her heritage. Besides, where had this lady been, under some rock? Why hadn't the lady seen any African-Americans before? Next was curiosity. Why did the lady ask the question of my student? After all, there were two other African-Americans in the class. Finally was a sense of duty. My student saw the encounter as a chance to fulfill her duty to present her race in a positive light. If she reacted in a negative way, she would give the lady a negative example by which she would paint all African-Americans in the future. For all my student knew, the lady might avoid future encounters with others who weren't like her.

Considering the life changing impact of her decision, my student allowed the lady to touch her hair. In my student's estimation, the touch took a bit longer than she'd anticipated but resulted in several other conversations about African-Americans and allowed my student to share her heritage, turning a rather awkward encounter into both a learning laboratory and a lasting friendship.

Friendship helps establish conditions essential to developing strong professional relationships and serves as a solid foundation for capitalizing on diversity in the workplace. According to a 2010 description published by Catherwood Library at Cornell University, workplace diversity is a people issue, focused on differences and similarities that people bring to an organization.

Usually defined broadly to include dimensions beyond those specified legally in equal opportunity and affirmative action non-discriminatory statutes, diversity is often interpreted to include the influence, identities, and perspectives that people bring, such as education, parental status, personality, and even eagerness to work with others unlike themselves.

Diversity isn't just about race, color, and the other more easily identifiable differences among us, it's about learning from others who are not the same, about dignity and respect for all, and about creating workplace environments and practices that encourage learning from others and capture the advantage of diverse perspectives.

If you continue to accept diversity and learn from others, you'll gain insight into those around you, which is one of the best reasons to join the Air Force. As you and your career evolve, I encourage you to cherish what you've learned by cataloguing your experiences.

CATALOGUE YOUR EXPERIENCES

We all have experiences and memories that can serve as inspiration to ourselves and others. Unfortunately, we don't often take stock of those events. Take time to catalogue your experiences because each story contains moments in your career that can serve as great examples to motivate and encourage others. Cataloging your experiences doesn't have to be complicated. You can use video recorders, diaries, or a simple recollection of the events that took place in your daily activities, but you'll need to keep track of the time spent at each base, in each unit, and with people you've met.

As time goes on, I'm sure you'll have an opportunity to draw on the knowledge and lessons you've catalogued to avoid repeating a mistake, to help you work through a situation, or to avert a catastrophe. For instance, in 2003 when I arrived at the SNCOA to begin my tenure, many instructors were nearing retirement. To offset their departures, a host of us rookies were brought in to ensure student projections were met and that there were no degradations due to a lack of qualified people to teach the curriculum.

Since the number of instructors was far greater than the amount of available space, I shared a small office with a fellow instructor who had a background vastly different from mine. He'd spent his time in the Air Force as a cop and in the computer and information technology field. I'd spent mine in transportation. Because I hadn't been arrested and didn't have the patience to understand the interworking of a machine that had the tendency of quitting when it got ready, regardless of what you're working on, I just knew I was in for some long days.

Surprisingly, after the first few months, we began to discover a few common interests but one seemed to take precedence: our eagerness to expand our knowledge. It wasn't long before we started to share ideas on how to improve one another's effectiveness in the classroom. From there, we ventured into other areas such as financial planning, proper uniform wear, and ultimately embarked upon a regular discussion of a couple of topics most would not dare: religion and politics.

Seeing these topics from two entirely different perspectives, we oftentimes found ourselves engaged in intense debates (PC for heated arguments) about the merits of something we'd either read or heard on the news and the decisions made by our leaders. On one occasion, I remember the conversation getting to the point where he abruptly got up and left the office and I, in hot pursuit, followed closely behind him still attempting to make one last key point he just had to hear.

If someone would have seen us storming down the hallway, he would have thought we were arch enemies heading to a spot designated for a duel. That was certainly not the case, this time. Because of the experiences I'd encountered at a particular base early in my career, I definitely had plenty of examples of what not to do when disagreements existed between a co-worker and me. Even though I knew my knowledge was superior to his on that particular point (at least I thought so), I didn't allow this conflict to be the foundation for the next one.

You see, our relationship centered on maintaining a great deal of mutual respect for each another. In doing so, we were able to express our own opinions and present points of view without the burden of having to upstage each other, requiring someone else to intervene in order for us to resolve the issue. As a result, we developed a great friendship that lasted throughout our assignment at the SNCOA and continues to this day.

Cataloging your experiences will also help you when you run into people from your previous assignments. For instance, since completing my instructor duty, I can't count the number of times I've been approached by someone who recognized me from that assignment.

While at the base exchange, four years after leaving the academy, I happened upon a gentleman who'd been in one of my classes. I learned he was still appreciative of some advice I'd given him shortly after he'd been passed over for a senior master sergeant promotion. My family was with me at the time so I'm glad the encounter was positive, but more importantly, the meeting showed how important cataloging your experiences can be. For him, seeing me was a reminder of how effective a word of encouragement can be in difficult times. He'd since been promoted to chief master sergeant.

The encounter also affirmed a concept I've embraced for a long time and encourage you to adopt as well: be careful how you treat people because chances are great that you will see them again. By cataloging your experiences, you'll also realize how many people you've established connections with. This pool of connections expands your ability to network.

NETWORK, NETWORK, NETWORK

We've all probably heard the old adage "It's not what you know, it's who you know." But, I can tell you this is among the truest statements anyone will ever tell you. On the surface, networking may seem like a bad thing, especially when your experience and qualifications are often emphasized as the main drivers to success. However, as you move up the ladder of success, someone usually has information you need and is in a position to decide whether you'll get a chance to exercise your abilities. Active networking will help you find and influence these people.

If you're an introvert, networking can be difficult. Still, I encourage you to spend at least 2 hours each week finding ways to connect with people. At most installations, a variety of organizations and community-sponsored events provide opportunities to shore up your contacts. At these functions and within your work center, you'll be able to get acquainted with plenty of people. I remember at one location the most popular off-duty activity was running.

Each month, there were numerous runs themed on everything from breast cancer awareness to rock and roll.

Although I wasn't able to participate much because of my health, I kept abreast of the event's theme and used it to spark conversations with the avid runners. From those conversations, we were able to connect and find out more about one another, our families, and other interests. Your results will be well worth the effort.

If you're an extrovert, as I am, networking will be a little easier. My experiences have convinced me that if you have the gift of gab, don't be shy. Use it to your advantage. Most people you'll run across in the Air Force will have at least some experiences in common with your own. A couple of good examples are basic training and technical school. Off-duty, the commissary and base exchange are excellent locations to network. In fact, nearly every time I visit the commissary with my wife, she says, "I'm not planning on spending all day in here, so don't spend too much time talking to everybody you know." On most days, I honor her wishes. On other days, I find it utterly impossible.

I also recommend you get involved with the other base activities that offer networking opportunities. Some of them are the Noncommissioned and Senior Noncommissioned Officer Associations, councils, groups, and clubs. Each of these organizations also offers avenues to become members of the board and to serve in various leadership capacities. If you are fortunate enough to earn appointment, you'll increase your exposure and strengthen your ability to network. In an article on business networking, Stephanie Speisman, offers a few additional tips for successful networking.

Keep in mind that networking is about being genuine and authentic, building trust and relationships, and seeing how you can help others. Your eagerness to do whatever you can to help others, especially your subordinates, will contribute directly to your own success and afford the intangible reward of knowing you've helped someone else in their time of need. Consistent expressions of unselfish acts toward others will also increase your influence.

Ask yourself what your goals are in participating in networking so that you will pick groups that will help you get what you are looking for. A variety of organizations are established to provide assistance to Air Force personnel and their families. Consider connecting with people assigned to the Force Support Squadron, Financial Service Center, Military and Civilian Personnel Offices and other organizations able to either provide what you seek or put you in contact with others that are able to help.

Ask open-ended questions in networking conversations. This means questions that ask who, what, where, when, and how as opposed to those that can be answered with a simple yes or no. This form of questioning opens up the discussion and shows listeners that you are interested in them. An added benefit is that your conversations will lead to a better understanding of each other and create an opportunity to further develop diverse, personal and/or professional relationships.

Be able to articulate what you are looking for and how others may help you. Your ability to articulate will prove very useful when you're seeking assistance from someone you know on behalf of a subordinate, peer, supervisor, your organization, etc.

Getting connected through networking is only one part of the equation; the other part is to use those connections to stay fit.

STAY FIT

We can all benefit from being in the best physical, spiritual, and emotional health possible. You can't be fully successful if each of these components is not fit because the body and mind have a knack for working in concert to help you accomplish the things you set out to achieve.

A lot has been written on the subject of physical fitness by experts with varying degrees, certifications, and experience on the topic. I won't go into the various theories here, but I encourage you to carefully review some of them to find ways to reach and maintain a higher level of physical fitness. The Air Force also has pretty stringent standards in place to ensure you incorporate a well-rounded physical fitness regimen into your lifestyle. In fact, your tenure will be contingent upon how well you meet these standards.

However, some people still find making time to work out a difficult challenge. Part of this challenge stems from a lack of motivation. To keep from falling into this same trap, consider the consequences. If you don't make time to maintain your physical fitness, you won't be able to do the things you like to do—drive that nice car, live in that beautiful home, send your kids to that super school, or take that vacation you've been planning because you'll be separated from the Air Force for failing your physical fitness test.

In addition to being physically fit, you'll need to be spiritually fit. Without attempting to sway you to a particular religion, I can tell you that identifying a higher power and accepting the reality that there is a being greater than we are will prove invaluable in any situation. I recall many times when I just couldn't figure out why things were happening the way they were and had difficulty staying motivated. In each of those valleys, I found refuge in knowing that God was nearby. It's hard to describe the feeling on paper, but I can still recall the moments where I found solace in knowing where to look for help.

Another important element to being fit is being emotionally healthy. To do so, you need to establish a strong support system. This support system will help keep you focused, provide an outlet, and buffer you through difficult times. I remember, on too many occasions, having to supervise personnel whose physical and emotional fitness were affected because they didn't have anyone to turn to in their times of need.

Mrs. Annie Tisdale, mother-in-law (seated) and Mrs. Ange Phillips, spouse (standing).

If nothing else, we all need someone with whom we can vent our frustrations and share our aspirations. This outlet is comparable to the opening on a tea kettle. When the steam cranks up, it finds its way to the top and releases into the air. For me, I was blessed with a wonderful wife who stood by my side through each of my ups and downs and twists and turns, especially during the numerous remotes (assignments to locations where I couldn't take my family) and deployments.

Not hindered by the time differences, we spent many nights (at my location) and days (at her location) on the phone and on the computer working our way through each situation and determining the best possible course of action and follow-up strategy. I was also blessed with my wonderful mother-in-law who was there for me and my family.

I oftentimes reminisce about when my mother-in-law rented out her home so she could travel out of state to live with my wife and two young sons while I spent a year at one of my three remote assignment locations.

At one particular location, several of my subordinates were going through trying times at home. I was able to offer assistance and encouragement to them because my own home life was stable. For example, I encountered one individual whose wife had given birth to their first child just six months before he arrived at the remote assignment. Him having been at the base for less than two months, I learned the family separation had already begun to take its toll on the person.

One day, I noticed him sitting at his desk staring into space. At first, I thought he was concentrating on something. But, when he didn't respond to my greeting and inquiry into whether he was alright, I knew it had to be something more serious. After getting his attention and posing the question again, he responded. Of course, my response to his telling me he was okay was, "Are you sure?" He hesitantly said, "Yes." Not wanting to cause a scene in the middle of the office where he sat among his two subordinates, I went on to my office and phoned his supervisor, whose office was no more than 10 feet from where we were having the conversation.

I believe his supervisor knew I'd be calling him because he answered the phone rather quickly and didn't seem too surprised I had concerns. In our conversation, I learned that the person's spouse had called, on several occasions, and expressed her displeasure with his being gone and had recently made a statement to the effect that she was going to take their child and disappear. Upon hearing what she planned to do, he simply shut down.

To make a long story short, we were able to gain approval for the individual to take his annual leave much earlier than normally authorized so he could get his affairs in order. Because I had the necessary support system at home, I was able to focus on providing him as much assistance as I could to get him through those trying times. For that, I thanked God continually for the ability to help him and for keeping things in order at my home during my absence.

Fortunately for this person and for me, I had the wherewithal to notice something just wasn't quite right and was able to intervene early enough to help him receive the necessary assistance. Ideally, whether going through something as dramatic as this situation or something on a smaller scale, to be successful in the Air Force, we each need to determine when to seek help.

SEEK HELP

Equally, if not more important, to your success in the Air Force, and any other endeavor, is the necessity to identify when to seek help. It goes without saying that sometimes the circumstances of events and consequences of situations may be beyond our capacity to deal with alone.

Such circumstances include, but certainly are not limited to, situations where your gut tells you that whatever is happening doesn't seem to follow the principles of good order and discipline and therefore, requires someone else's help to obtain resolution, remedy, or elimination.

The Department of Defense is a large organization and there are incidents of fraud, waste, and abuse. However, no one has enough power over you to do something illegal or immoral. If you find yourself in a situation where someone of authority orders you to do something you know is wrong or is abusing you, say something to someone immediately! Go to your commander, first sergeant, supervisor, chaplain, the Inspector General (IG), or anyone else who can help address the situation. Additionally, if you witness a problem, report it with the same since of urgency.

Looking back on all of the things I went through, all of people I met, and all of the opportunities afforded me, I am thankful for my experiences. In a larger sense, I am even grateful things turned out the way they did. Could I have hoped for outcomes in some areas to have turned out a bit more in my favor than they did? Absolutely! Are there some things I did that I wish I could have done a little differently? Sure.

Overall though, I couldn't have chosen a better career path than to have become an enlisted member of the Air Force. As an expression of my commitment, I did all I could do to be successful. When you've done all you can do to ensure you're successful and have devoted the time and effort needed to help others succeed, recharge your drive and motivation to reach greater heights by taking time to reflect.

TAKE TIME TO REFLECT

Careful reflection on things that have happened to you is essential to your success. Those times in your life and career when you faced insurmountable challenges actually serve as constant reminders of where your motivation to reach greater heights comes from.

Throughout my career, I spent countless hours and expended lots of energy attempting to convince others to accept my ideas for improving processes and procedures only to have many of them dismissed outright, sometimes without a small bit of consideration. On other occasions, I challenged organizations with long-standing policies I felt placed unnecessary barriers in the way of my ability to meet my personal and professional goals and hindered my unit's ability to accomplish its mission.

Having chosen to go up against the status quo, you'd think I simply stayed focused on achieving the desired outcomes without a shadow of a doubt. Not quite. There were times when I began to second guess the actions I'd taken to facilitate the changes I sought. Questions sometimes entered my mind like: Why didn't I just work within the existing guidelines? Why can't I accept the supervisor's explanation why this regulatory provision prohibits what I'm attempting to obtain for my subordinates?

Each time, the moment I began to think like that, I'd assure myself that I needed to follow through with my plan so I could make things better or achieve what I sought out to accomplish.

No matter how great the feat, if you keep your head up and take time to reflect, you'll indeed successfully meet each and every challenge and gain experience from your journey that will definitely prepare you to face the next one.

AUTHOR'S NOTE

If, after the first time you read this book, you are not totally convinced that this practical guide will help you succeed in your Air Force career, read it or portions of it again and again. Chances are great that you'll find the inspiration needed to continue your journey toward achieving the level of success you seek. Learning what to do is just part of the equation. Your success requires you to put what you've learned into action.

Don't be surprised if you receive a bit of push back after you ask some tough questions or challenge the long-standing status quo. I say this not to portray that I have such infinite wisdom but to raise your awareness of the fact that enlisted personnel aren't usually called upon to exercise their critical thinking abilities, even though I believe we have plenty to offer. Instead, traditionally, enlisted personnel engage after the key decisions have been made, a model that produces situations where the need to employ the necessary knowledge and skills comes after things have gone wrong. If you find this type of forethought appealing, I encourage you to read my next book entitled: *STRATEGIC LEADERSHIP: The Inside Scoop (A Senior Enlisted Leader's Perspective)*.

I'm sure you'll be glad you did!

ADDITIONAL INSIGHT

Throughout my career, I've had the opportunity to live and work alongside some of the most intelligent and accomplished people. Here are just a few of their thoughts on what you can do to be successful in the Air Force.

"Success in the Air Force is having the ability to know when and how to use the "tools" learned throughout life like respect, staying focused on the task at hand, knowing when to express your disagreement with the boss, and the willingness to stand up for what's right, regardless of the consequences."

Ange M. Phillips, SrA, USAF
Morse Code Journeyman (1N2), 1988-1994

"Success in the Air Force is developing a plan to do things when they need to be done and not allowing procrastination to be the constant reason why you didn't reach your goals."

Kathy B. Jackson, MSgt, USAF
Aviation Resource Management (1C0), 2012

"Determination, Discipline and Dedication are the key components to being successful in the United States Air Force. Determination promotes purpose and the drive to change. Discipline helps

maintain focus on goals even when obstacles or challenges arise. Dedication keeps focus on goals even when an opportunity is not immediately presented."

Romonda P. Griffin, SSgt, USAF
Transportation (2T0),
1991-2002 Ph.D. candidate

"The key to having a successful Air Force career is to master your job, diligently pursue further education, and take on some base and/or community activities that allow you to lead. All of these factors are in one's control; ironically doing these things not only prepares you for success in the Air Force, but also in your next career."

Herbert H. Schlecht, CMSgt, USAF, (Ret.)
Transportation (2T0), 1982-2008

"Most successful people I know have drive, determination, and strong convictions. They are also confident, charismatic and are able to work well with others. These are all signs of a good leader."

Kevin McFarland, MSgt, USAF, (Ret.)
Logistics Plans (2G), 1986-2010

"The key to having a successful Air Force career is adhering to morals, values and attitude instilled in you as a child by your parents and/or grandparents; coupled with the love and support of your spouse...all things are possible. The sky is the limit!"

Tony C. Skinner, CMSgt, USAF
Material Management (2S), 2012

"To be successful in the Air Force, you have to set goals and do everything in your power to accomplish those goals."

Curlie Alexander, CMSgt, USAF
Logistics Plans (2G), 2012

"To be successful in the Air Force, you should work hard and always continue to learn and grow through college education. You can learn a lot from your leaders, co-workers, supervisors, friends and family. Also, be a good listener and always be fair."

Charles E. Irvin MSgt, USAF (Ret.)
Transportation (2T0), 1986-2011

"To be successful in the Air Force, "Pick a Champion." Find someone who has done what you want to accomplish-a mentor- and duplicate it. Don't follow mentor candidates blindly; interview them to ensure your morals, goals, beliefs and aspirations align with theirs before allowing anyone to help you reach the next level."

Darnell M. Ingram, TSgt, USAF
Transportation (2T0), 2012

REFERENCES

Air Force Benefits Descriptions. (2012). Retrieved 15 January, 2012 from www.airforce.com.

Air Force Core Values. (2012). Retrieved 15 January, 2012 from www.airforce.com.

Air Force Pamphlet 36-2241, *Professional Development Guide* (2012). Retrieved 15 January, 2012 from www.e-publishing.af.mil.

Airman's Creed (2007) Retrieved 22 January, 2012 from www.airforce.com.

Conflict. (2012) MeriamWebster.com. A Britannica Company. Retrieved 6 February, 2012 www.meriamwebster.com.

Diversity. (2012). Retrieved 3 February, 2012 from www.meriamwebster.com.

Sound judgment. (2012). Retrieved 5 February, 2012 from www.freedictionary.com.

Speisman, S. (2009). *10 Tips for Successful Business Networking.* Retrieved 17 January, 2012 from <u>www.businessknowhow.com</u>.

Workplace Diversity. Itchaca, NY: Cornell University ILR.